How High Am I?

A JOURNAL

**GENIUS IDEAS ✸ DRAWINGS
STUFF YOU DON'T WANT TO FORGET**

CHRONICLE BOOKS
SAN FRANCISCO

ISBN 978-0-8118-7443-4

Manufactured in China
Design by Michael Morris

10 9 8 7

Chronicle Books LLC
680 Second Street
San Francisco, CA 94107
www.chroniclebooks.com

Weed—isn't it wonderful?

Seriously. Listening to music, eating chili-cheese nachos—anything and everything—feels pretty awesome after a toke or two. And wow! Life is amazing. Thanks to our kind green bud, life's profundity reveals itself everywhere in all situations: hiking in nature, watching the sunset, sitting on the couch, playing video games, or getting your frolf on. Need weed say more?

Sometimes pot is so wonderful, it's hard to stay focused. It's easy to forget all those fleeting thoughts, genius ideas, big questions, and random points of inspiration. Hey, you know what sounds totally good right now? Tacos, stuffed with macaroni and cheese . . . Wait, what were we just talking about? Oh, yeah. Deep thoughts. That's what this journal is for. Use it to doodle and record notes about your high—including method (joint, bong, vaporizer, edibles) and strain (indica, sativa, mix). Jot down reminders and miscellaneous notes, like your stoned daydreams, big project ideas, or top ten lists of the best things ever, or lists of words that sound funny when you say them over and over. Top ten. Top ten. Topten topten toptentoptentopten.

Top ten. What? Remembering is hard. Fortunately, you don't have to do it anymore. Now, when you have those really insightful, life-changing ideas, write them down for safekeeping here. This journal will do all your important remembering for you. So put on some tunes, grab your journal, and kick back. All you have to do is enjoy the high life.

If you smoke a lot of pot you know that it makes you ask many deep and not-so-deep questions. Some of those questions are about the meaning of life; some are about what would taste good with pancake syrup; and some are about the magical weed itself. Here are the answers to your burning pot questions:

What is marijuana, pot, weed, ganja, reefer? And where do they all come from?

They come from Gene, the slightly creepy guy with the ponytail and pet ferret in apartment 4A. Ha ha. No, but seriously, these are all terms for cannabis, a plant that has been cultivated worldwide for thousands and thousands of years. Cannabis is believed to be native to Central Asia and it is said that Chinese cultures were growing it as far back as 6,000 B.C. No joke. Today, different varieties of the plant grow all over the world, and are used for a wide range of purposes—industrial, medicinal, spiritual, and recreational.

Marijuana, pot, weed, ganja, reefer—and a number of other terms—all refer to the dried flowers (or buds) and leaves of the mature female cannabis plant, which induce physiological and psychoactive effects when smoked, vaporized, or snarfed down in brownie form. This type of cannabis plant is used to get high, baked, stoned, and totally ripped.

Hemp is another (nonpsychoactive) variety of the cannabis plant. It is harvested to make fiber which is used to make paper, fabric, rope, and all kinds of industrial goods. This kind of cannabis will not get you high, so don't try to smoke it. Eating a hemp granola bar or using hemp shampoo will not get you buzzed.

Why does marijuana make me feel high?

It's science, dude. Cannabis contains hundreds of chemicals, some of which are known as cannabinoids. THC (delta-9-tetrahydrocannabinol) is the main mind-altering cannabinoid in marijuana that is responsible for the sensation of feeling "high." Basically, when you spark a doob, THC travels through your bloodstream to your brain and immune system where it interacts with specific nerve cells responsible for various mental and physical functions (including coordination, memory, appetite, and laughter). THC binds with the membranes of these nerve cells, setting off a series of cellular reactions that result in hunger and party time. Crazy thing about it all is that the human body produces its own THC-like chemical called anandamide, so basically THC mimics the actions and effects of this natural-occuring cannabinoid.

CBD (cannabidiol) is another active cannabinoid in marijuana that can increase or decrease the effects of THC. "Cannabidiol" is also really fun to say when you're stoned.

How come I feel different highs?

That's the beauty of weed, man. Just as you can never step in the same river twice, so you can never blaze the same blunt. Every high is different.

How you feel depends on a variety of factors, such as the amount of THC (and the other sixty or so cannabinoids) in that specific strain of marijuana, the method of consumption, and your general disposition.

Also, keep in mind that there are three different species of the cannabis plant—indica, sativa, and ruderalis—all of which produce different kinds of highs. Indica tends to have a heavier, muscle-relaxing, sedative effect or "body stone." Sativa tends to be more energizing and uplifting—more of a "head high." Ruderalis has a low level of THC and is not usually consumed as is, but because it withstands harsh weather, it's good for cross-breeding with indica and sativa.

Every strain is different, and there are regional variations. That's why the pot you smoke while on vacation with your parents in Mexico makes you want to get a hair wrap, and the pot you smoke in Yosemite makes you want to eat marshmallows and uncooked ramen packets. Mmmm. Marshmallows.

How High Am I?

- ○ 1 Not at all
- ○ 2 Feeling a buzz
- ○ 3 Getting kinda toasty
- ○ 4 Pretty baked
- ○ 5 Life is beautiful
- ○ 6 Mmmmm, munchies
- ○ 7 Whoa! High as a kite
- ○ 8 Totally stoned
- ○ 9 What was I doing again?
- ○ 10 Have you ever really looked at your hand?

DATE	TIME	LOCATION

High notes (METHOD / STRAIN / CHARACTERISTICS):

_____

_____

_____

What am I feeling?

_____

_____

_____

What am I doing? / What am I eating?

_____

_____

_____

_____

What can I absolutely not forget, no matter what?

_____

_____

_____

Genius idea:

_____

_____

Big question:

_____

_____

_____

Doodle

The first record of marijuana's medicinal properties dates as far back as 28 B.C. in an ancient Chinese pharmacopeia. Marijuana is still used today to alleviate pain, stimulate appetite, and treat a wide variety of ailments.

How High Am I?

- ○ 1 Not at all
- ○ 2 Feeling a buzz
- ○ 3 Getting kinda toasty
- ○ 4 Pretty baked
- ○ 5 Life is beautiful
- ○ 6 Mmmmm, munchies
- ○ 7 Whoa! High as a kite
- ○ 8 Totally stoned
- ○ 9 What was I doing again?
- ○ 10 Have you ever really looked at your hand?

DATE	TIME	LOCATION

High notes (METHOD / STRAIN / CHARACTERISTICS):

_____

_____

_____

What am I feeling?

_____

_____

_____

What am I doing? / What am I eating?

_____

_____

_____

What can I absolutely not forget, no matter what?

_____

_____

_____

Genius idea:

_____

_____

_____

Big question:

_____

_____

_____

Doodle

It's high time to laugh every day. Studies show that it's good for you. Laughing relieves tension and stress, increases blood flow, boosts the immune system, and triggers the release of endorphins.

How High Am I?

○ 1 Not at all
○ 2 Feeling a buzz
○ 3 Getting kinda toasty
○ 4 Pretty baked
○ 5 Life is beautiful

○ 6 Mmmmm, munchies
○ 7 Whoa! High as a kite
○ 8 Totally stoned
○ 9 What was I doing again?
○10 Have you ever really looked at your hand?

DATE	TIME	LOCATION

High notes (METHOD / STRAIN / CHARACTERISTICS):

_____

_____

_____

What am I feeling?

_____

_____

_____

What am I doing? / What am I eating?

_____

_____

_____

What can I absolutely not forget, no matter what?

_____

_____

_____

Genius idea:

_____

_____

_____

Big question:

_____

_____

_____

Doodle

Marijuana has been used in religious and spiritual practices throughout history and is said to enhance communication with the spirit world.

How High Am I?

- ○ 1 Not at all
- ○ 2 Feeling a buzz
- ○ 3 Getting kinda toasty
- ○ 4 Pretty baked
- ○ 5 Life is beautiful
- ○ 6 Mmmmm, munchies
- ○ 7 Whoa! High as a kite
- ○ 8 Totally stoned
- ○ 9 What was I doing again?
- ○ 10 Have you ever really looked at your hand?

DATE	TIME	LOCATION

High notes (METHOD / STRAIN / CHARACTERISTICS):

_____

_____

_____

What am I feeling?

_____

_____

_____

What am I doing? / What am I eating?

_____

_____

_____

What can I absolutely not forget, no matter what?

_____

_____

_____

Genius idea:

_____

_____

_____

Big question:

_____

_____

_____

Doodle

It's high time to break your routine. Try something different and unusual.
Do something that takes you out of your comfort zone. Challenge yourself.
Learn something new.

How High Am I?

- ○ 1 Not at all
- ○ 2 Feeling a buzz
- ○ 3 Getting kinda toasty
- ○ 4 Pretty baked
- ○ 5 Life is beautiful
- ○ 6 Mmmmm, munchies
- ○ 7 Whoa! High as a kite
- ○ 8 Totally stoned
- ○ 9 What was I doing again?
- ○ 10 Have you ever really looked at your hand?

DATE	TIME	LOCATION

High notes (METHOD / STRAIN / CHARACTERISTICS):

_____

_____

_____

What am I feeling?

_____

_____

_____

What am I doing? / What am I eating?

_____

_____

_____

What can I absolutely not forget, no matter what?

_____

_____

_____

Genius idea:

_____

_____

_____

Big question:

_____

_____

_____

Doodle

How High Am I?

- ○ 1 Not at all
- ○ 2 Feeling a buzz
- ○ 3 Getting kinda toasty
- ○ 4 Pretty baked
- ○ 5 Life is beautiful
- ○ 6 Mmmmm, munchies
- ○ 7 Whoa! High as a kite
- ○ 8 Totally stoned
- ○ 9 What was I doing again?
- ○ 10 Have you ever really looked at your hand?

DATE	TIME	LOCATION

High notes (METHOD / STRAIN / CHARACTERISTICS):

_____

_____

_____

What am I feeling?

_____

_____

_____

What am I doing? / What am I eating?

_____

_____

_____

What can I absolutely not forget, no matter what?

_____

_____

_____

Genius idea:

_____

_____

_____

Big question:

_____

_____

_____

Doodle

The average life of a taste bud cell is ten days, so next time you get the munchies, pay attention to the details: the different tastes, smells, and textures of what you're eating.

How High Am I?

- ○ 1 Not at all
- ○ 2 Feeling a buzz
- ○ 3 Getting kinda toasty
- ○ 4 Pretty baked
- ○ 5 Life is beautiful
- ○ 6 Mmmmm, munchies
- ○ 7 Whoa! High as a kite
- ○ 8 Totally stoned
- ○ 9 What was I doing again?
- ○ 10 Have you ever really looked at your hand?

DATE	TIME	LOCATION

High notes (METHOD / STRAIN / CHARACTERISTICS):

_____

_____

_____

What am I feeling?

_____

_____

_____

What am I doing? / What am I eating?

_____

_____

_____

What can I absolutely not forget, no matter what?

_____

_____

_____

Genius idea:

_____

_____

_____

Big question:

_____

_____

_____

Doodle

Store your weed in an airtight jar in a cool dark place to prevent your buds from drying out.

How High Am I?

- ○ 1 Not at all
- ○ 2 Feeling a buzz
- ○ 3 Getting kinda toasty
- ○ 4 Pretty baked
- ○ 5 Life is beautiful
- ○ 6 Mmmmm, munchies
- ○ 7 Whoa! High as a kite
- ○ 8 Totally stoned
- ○ 9 What was I doing again?
- ○ 10 Have you ever really looked at your hand?

| DATE | TIME | LOCATION |

High notes (METHOD / STRAIN / CHARACTERISTICS):

_____

_____

_____

What am I feeling?

_____

_____

_____

What am I doing? / What am I eating?

_____

_____

_____

What can I absolutely not forget, no matter what?

_____

_____

_____

Genius idea:

_____

_____

_____

Big question:

_____

_____

_____

Doodle

Hashish is a product of marijuana and is made by collecting and compressing the THC-rich resin from the buds of the female cannabis plant.

How High Am I?

- ○ 1 Not at all
- ○ 2 Feeling a buzz
- ○ 3 Getting kinda toasty
- ○ 4 Pretty baked
- ○ 5 Life is beautiful
- ○ 6 Mmmmm, munchies
- ○ 7 Whoa! High as a kite
- ○ 8 Totally stoned
- ○ 9 What was I doing again?
- ○ 10 Have you ever really looked at your hand?

DATE	TIME	LOCATION

High notes (METHOD / STRAIN / CHARACTERISTICS):

_____

_____

_____

What am I feeling?

_____

_____

_____

What am I doing? / What am I eating?

_____

_____

_____

_____

What can I absolutely not forget, no matter what?

_____

_____

_____

Genius idea:

_____

_____

_____

Big question:

_____

_____

_____

Doodle

The first record of marijuana's medicinal properties dates as far back as 28 B.C. in an ancient Chinese pharmacopeia. Marijuana is still used today to alleviate pain, stimulate appetite, and treat a wide variety of ailments.

How High Am I?

- ○ 1 Not at all
- ○ 2 Feeling a buzz
- ○ 3 Getting kinda toasty
- ○ 4 Pretty baked
- ○ 5 Life is beautiful
- ○ 6 Mmmmm, munchies
- ○ 7 Whoa! High as a kite
- ○ 8 Totally stoned
- ○ 9 What was I doing again?
- ○10 Have you ever really looked at your hand?

DATE	TIME	LOCATION

High notes (METHOD / STRAIN / CHARACTERISTICS):

_____

_____

_____

What am I feeling?

_____

_____

_____

What am I doing? / What am I eating?

_____

_____

_____

What can I absolutely not forget, no matter what?

_____

_____

_____

Genius idea:

_____

_____

_____

Big question:

_____

_____

_____

Doodle

It's high time to laugh every day. Studies show that it's good for you. Laughing relieves tension and stress, increases blood flow, boosts the immune system, and triggers the release of endorphins.

How High Am I?

- ○ 1 Not at all
- ○ 2 Feeling a buzz
- ○ 3 Getting kinda toasty
- ○ 4 Pretty baked
- ○ 5 Life is beautiful

- ○ 6 Mmmmm, munchies
- ○ 7 Whoa! High as a kite
- ○ 8 Totally stoned
- ○ 9 What was I doing again?
- ○ 10 Have you ever really looked at your hand?

DATE	TIME	LOCATION

High notes (METHOD / STRAIN / CHARACTERISTICS):

_____

_____

_____

What am I feeling?

_____

_____

_____

What am I doing? / What am I eating?

_____

_____

_____

What can I absolutely not forget, no matter what?

_____

_____

_____

Genius idea:

_____

_____

_____

Big question:

_____

_____

_____

Doodle

Marijuana has been used in religious and spiritual practices throughout history and is said to enhance communication with the spirit world.

How High Am I?

- ○ 1 Not at all
- ○ 2 Feeling a buzz
- ○ 3 Getting kinda toasty
- ○ 4 Pretty baked
- ○ 5 Life is beautiful
- ○ 6 Mmmmm, munchies
- ○ 7 Whoa! High as a kite
- ○ 8 Totally stoned
- ○ 9 What was I doing again?
- ○ 10 Have you ever really looked at your hand?

| DATE | TIME | LOCATION |

High notes (METHOD / STRAIN / CHARACTERISTICS):

_____

_____

_____

What am I feeling?

_____

_____

_____

What am I doing? / What am I eating?

_____

_____

_____

What can I absolutely not forget, no matter what?

_____
_____
_____

Genius idea:

_____
_____
_____

Big question:

_____
_____
_____

Doodle

It's high time to break your routine. Try something different and unusual. Do something that takes you out of your comfort zone. Challenge yourself. Learn something new.

How High Am I?

- ○ 1 Not at all
- ○ 2 Feeling a buzz
- ○ 3 Getting kinda toasty
- ○ 4 Pretty baked
- ○ 5 Life is beautiful
- ○ 6 Mmmmm, munchies
- ○ 7 Whoa! High as a kite
- ○ 8 Totally stoned
- ○ 9 What was I doing again?
- ○ 10 Have you ever really looked at your hand?

DATE	TIME	LOCATION

High notes (METHOD / STRAIN / CHARACTERISTICS):

_____

_____

_____

What am I feeling?

_____

_____

_____

What am I doing? / What am I eating?

_____

_____

_____

_____

What can I absolutely not forget, no matter what?

_____

_____

_____

Genius idea:

_____

_____

_____

Big question:

_____

_____

_____

Doodle

THC is the primary mind-altering chemical in marijuana and is most concentrated in the buds of the female cannabis plant.

How High Am I?

- ○ 1 Not at all
- ○ 2 Feeling a buzz
- ○ 3 Getting kinda toasty
- ○ 4 Pretty baked
- ○ 5 Life is beautiful
- ○ 6 Mmmmm, munchies
- ○ 7 Whoa! High as a kite
- ○ 8 Totally stoned
- ○ 9 What was I doing again?
- ○ 10 Have you ever really looked at your hand?

DATE	TIME	LOCATION

High notes (METHOD / STRAIN / CHARACTERISTICS):

_____

_____

_____

What am I feeling?

_____

_____

_____

What am I doing? / What am I eating?

_____

_____

_____

What can I absolutely not forget, no matter what?

_____
_____
_____

Genius idea:

_____
_____
_____

Big question:

_____
_____
_____

Doodle

The average life of a taste bud cell is ten days, so next time you get the munchies, pay attention to the details: the different tastes, smells, and textures of what you're eating.

How High Am I?

- ○ 1 Not at all
- ○ 2 Feeling a buzz
- ○ 3 Getting kinda toasty
- ○ 4 Pretty baked
- ○ 5 Life is beautiful
- ○ 6 Mmmmm, munchies
- ○ 7 Whoa! High as a kite
- ○ 8 Totally stoned
- ○ 9 What was I doing again?
- ○ 10 Have you ever really looked at your hand?

DATE	TIME	LOCATION

High notes (METHOD / STRAIN / CHARACTERISTICS):

_____

_____

_____

What am I feeling?

_____

_____

_____

What am I doing? / What am I eating?

_____

_____

_____

What can I absolutely not forget, no matter what?

_____
_____
_____

Genius idea:

_____
_____
_____

Big question:

_____
_____
_____

Doodle

Store your weed in an airtight jar in a cool dark place to prevent your buds from drying out.

How High Am I?

- ○ 1 Not at all
- ○ 2 Feeling a buzz
- ○ 3 Getting kinda toasty
- ○ 4 Pretty baked
- ○ 5 Life is beautiful
- ○ 6 Mmmmm, munchies
- ○ 7 Whoa! High as a kite
- ○ 8 Totally stoned
- ○ 9 What was I doing again?
- ○ 10 Have you ever really looked at your hand?

DATE	TIME	LOCATION

High notes (METHOD / STRAIN / CHARACTERISTICS):

_____

_____

_____

What am I feeling?

_____

_____

_____

What am I doing? / What am I eating?

_____

_____

_____

_____

What can I absolutely not forget, no matter what?

Genius idea:

Big question:

Doodle

Hashish is a product of marijuana and is made by collecting and compressing the THC-rich resin from the buds of the female cannabis plant.

How High Am I?

○ 1 Not at all
○ 2 Feeling a buzz
○ 3 Getting kinda toasty
○ 4 Pretty baked
○ 5 Life is beautiful

○ 6 Mmmmm, munchies
○ 7 Whoa! High as a kite
○ 8 Totally stoned
○ 9 What was I doing again?
○10 Have you ever really looked at your hand?

| DATE | TIME | LOCATION |

High notes (METHOD / STRAIN / CHARACTERISTICS):

_____
_____
_____

What am I feeling?

_____
_____
_____

What am I doing? / What am I eating?

_____
_____
_____

What can I absolutely not forget, no matter what?

_____

_____

_____

Genius idea:

_____

_____

_____

Big question:

_____

_____

_____

Doodle

The first record of marijuana's medicinal properties dates as far back as 28 B.C. in an ancient Chinese pharmacopeia. Marijuana is still used today to alleviate pain, stimulate appetite, and treat a wide variety of ailments.

How High Am I?

- ○ 1 Not at all
- ○ 2 Feeling a buzz
- ○ 3 Getting kinda toasty
- ○ 4 Pretty baked
- ○ 5 Life is beautiful
- ○ 6 Mmmmm, munchies
- ○ 7 Whoa! High as a kite
- ○ 8 Totally stoned
- ○ 9 What was I doing again?
- ○ 10 Have you ever really looked at your hand?

DATE	TIME	LOCATION

High notes (METHOD / STRAIN / CHARACTERISTICS):

_____

_____

_____

What am I feeling?

_____

_____

_____

What am I doing? / What am I eating?

_____

_____

_____

What can I absolutely not forget, no matter what?

_____

_____

_____

Genius idea:

_____

_____

_____

Big question:

_____

_____

_____

Doodle

It's high time to laugh every day. Studies show that it's good for you.
Laughing relieves tension and stress, increases blood flow, boosts the
immune system, and triggers the release of endorphins.

How High Am I?

- ○ 1 Not at all
- ○ 2 Feeling a buzz
- ○ 3 Getting kinda toasty
- ○ 4 Pretty baked
- ○ 5 Life is beautiful
- ○ 6 Mmmmm, munchies
- ○ 7 Whoa! High as a kite
- ○ 8 Totally stoned
- ○ 9 What was I doing again?
- ○ 10 Have you ever really looked at your hand?

DATE	TIME	LOCATION

High notes (METHOD / STRAIN / CHARACTERISTICS):

_____
_____
_____

What am I feeling?

_____
_____
_____

What am I doing? / What am I eating?

_____
_____
_____

What can I absolutely not forget, no matter what?

_____

_____

_____

Genius idea:

_____

_____

_____

Big question:

_____

_____

_____

Doodle

Marijuana has been used in religious and spiritual practices throughout history and is said to enhance communication with the spirit world.

How High Am I?

○ 1 Not at all
○ 2 Feeling a buzz
○ 3 Getting kinda toasty
○ 4 Pretty baked
○ 5 Life is beautiful

○ 6 Mmmmm, munchies
○ 7 Whoa! High as a kite
○ 8 Totally stoned
○ 9 What was I doing again?
○ 10 Have you ever really looked at your hand?

DATE	TIME	LOCATION

High notes (METHOD / STRAIN / CHARACTERISTICS):

_____
_____
_____

What am I feeling?

_____
_____
_____

What am I doing? / What am I eating?

_____
_____
_____

What can I absolutely not forget, no matter what?

_____

_____

_____

Genius idea:

_____

_____

_____

Big question:

_____

_____

_____

Doodle

It's high time to break your routine. Try something different and unusual. Do something that takes you out of your comfort zone. Challenge yourself. Learn something new.

How High Am I?

- ○ 1 Not at all
- ○ 2 Feeling a buzz
- ○ 3 Getting kinda toasty
- ○ 4 Pretty baked
- ○ 5 Life is beautiful
- ○ 6 Mmmmm, munchies
- ○ 7 Whoa! High as a kite
- ○ 8 Totally stoned
- ○ 9 What was I doing again?
- ○ 10 Have you ever really looked at your hand?

DATE	TIME	LOCATION

High notes (METHOD / STRAIN / CHARACTERISTICS):

_____

_____

_____

What am I feeling?

_____

_____

_____

What am I doing? / What am I eating?

_____

_____

_____

What can I absolutely not forget, no matter what?

_____

_____

_____

Genius idea:

_____

_____

_____

Big question:

_____

_____

_____

Doodle

THC is the primary mind-altering chemical in marijuana and is most concentrated in the buds of the female cannabis plant.

How High Am I?

- ○ 1 Not at all
- ○ 2 Feeling a buzz
- ○ 3 Getting kinda toasty
- ○ 4 Pretty baked
- ○ 5 Life is beautiful
- ○ 6 Mmmmm, munchies
- ○ 7 Whoa! High as a kite
- ○ 8 Totally stoned
- ○ 9 What was I doing again?
- ○ 10 Have you ever really looked at your hand?

DATE	TIME	LOCATION

High notes (METHOD / STRAIN / CHARACTERISTICS):

_____

_____

_____

What am I feeling?

_____

_____

_____

What am I doing? / What am I eating?

_____

_____

_____

What can I absolutely not forget, no matter what?

_____

_____

_____

Genius idea:

_____

_____

_____

Big question:

_____

_____

_____

Doodle

The average life of a taste bud cell is ten days, so next time you get the munchies, pay attention to the details: the different tastes, smells, and textures of what you're eating.

How High Am I?

- ○ 1 Not at all
- ○ 2 Feeling a buzz
- ○ 3 Getting kinda toasty
- ○ 4 Pretty baked
- ○ 5 Life is beautiful
- ○ 6 Mmmmm, munchies
- ○ 7 Whoa! High as a kite
- ○ 8 Totally stoned
- ○ 9 What was I doing again?
- ○ 10 Have you ever really looked at your hand?

DATE	TIME	LOCATION

High notes (METHOD / STRAIN / CHARACTERISTICS):

_____

_____

_____

What am I feeling?

_____

_____

_____

What am I doing? / What am I eating?

_____

_____

_____

What can I absolutely not forget, no matter what?

_____
_____
_____

Genius idea:

_____
_____
_____

Big question:

_____
_____
_____

Doodle

Store your weed in an airtight jar in a cool dark place to prevent your buds from drying out.

How High Am I?

- ○ 1 Not at all
- ○ 2 Feeling a buzz
- ○ 3 Getting kinda toasty
- ○ 4 Pretty baked
- ○ 5 Life is beautiful
- ○ 6 Mmmmm, munchies
- ○ 7 Whoa! High as a kite
- ○ 8 Totally stoned
- ○ 9 What was I doing again?
- ○ 10 Have you ever really looked at your hand?

DATE	TIME	LOCATION

High notes (METHOD / STRAIN / CHARACTERISTICS):

_____

_____

_____

What am I feeling?

_____

_____

_____

What am I doing? / What am I eating?

_____

_____

_____

What can I absolutely not forget, no matter what?

_____

_____

_____

Genius idea:

_____

_____

_____

Big question:

_____

_____

_____

Doodle

Hashish is a product of marijuana and is made by collecting and compressing the THC-rich resin from the buds of the female cannabis plant.

How High Am I?

- ○ 1 Not at all
- ○ 2 Feeling a buzz
- ○ 3 Getting kinda toasty
- ○ 4 Pretty baked
- ○ 5 Life is beautiful
- ○ 6 Mmmmm, munchies
- ○ 7 Whoa! High as a kite
- ○ 8 Totally stoned
- ○ 9 What was I doing again?
- ○ 10 Have you ever really looked at your hand?

| DATE | TIME | LOCATION |

High notes (METHOD / STRAIN / CHARACTERISTICS):

_____

_____

_____

What am I feeling?

_____

_____

_____

What am I doing? / What am I eating?

_____

_____

_____

What can I absolutely not forget, no matter what?

_____

_____

_____

Genius idea:

_____

_____

_____

Big question:

_____

_____

_____

Doodle

The first record of marijuana's medicinal properties dates as far back as 28 B.C. in an ancient Chinese pharmacopeia. Marijuana is still used today to alleviate pain, stimulate appetite, and treat a wide variety of ailments.

How High Am I?

○ 1 Not at all
○ 2 Feeling a buzz
○ 3 Getting kinda toasty
○ 4 Pretty baked
○ 5 Life is beautiful

○ 6 Mmmmm, munchies
○ 7 Whoa! High as a kite
○ 8 Totally stoned
○ 9 What was I doing again?
○ 10 Have you ever really looked at your hand?

DATE	TIME	LOCATION

High notes (METHOD / STRAIN / CHARACTERISTICS):

_____
_____
_____

What am I feeling?

_____
_____
_____

What am I doing? / What am I eating?

_____
_____
_____

What can I absolutely not forget, no matter what?

_____

_____

_____

Genius idea:

_____

_____

_____

Big question:

_____

_____

_____

Doodle

It's high time to laugh every day. Studies show that it's good for you.
Laughing relieves tension and stress, increases blood flow, boosts the
immune system, and triggers the release of endorphins.

How High Am I?

○ 1 Not at all
○ 2 Feeling a buzz
○ 3 Getting kinda toasty
○ 4 Pretty baked
○ 5 Life is beautiful
○ 6 Mmmmm, munchies
○ 7 Whoa! High as a kite
○ 8 Totally stoned
○ 9 What was I doing again?
○ 10 Have you ever really looked at your hand?

DATE	TIME	LOCATION

High notes (METHOD / STRAIN / CHARACTERISTICS):

_____

_____

_____

What am I feeling?

_____

_____

_____

What am I doing? / What am I eating?

_____

_____

_____

What can I absolutely not forget, no matter what?

_____

_____

_____

Genius idea:

_____

_____

_____

Big question:

_____

_____

_____

Doodle

Marijuana has been used in religious and spiritual practices throughout history and is said to enhance communication with the spirit world.

How High Am I?

- ○ 1 Not at all
- ○ 2 Feeling a buzz
- ○ 3 Getting kinda toasty
- ○ 4 Pretty baked
- ○ 5 Life is beautiful
- ○ 6 Mmmmm, munchies
- ○ 7 Whoa! High as a kite
- ○ 8 Totally stoned
- ○ 9 What was I doing again?
- ○ 10 Have you ever really looked at your hand?

DATE	TIME	LOCATION

High notes (METHOD / STRAIN / CHARACTERISTICS):

_____

_____

_____

What am I feeling?

_____

_____

_____

What am I doing? / What am I eating?

_____

_____

_____

What can I absolutely not forget, no matter what?

_____

_____

_____

Genius idea:

_____

_____

_____

Big question:

_____

_____

_____

Doodle

It's high time to break your routine. Try something different and unusual. Do something that takes you out of your comfort zone. Challenge yourself. Learn something new.

How High Am I?

- ○ 1 Not at all
- ○ 2 Feeling a buzz
- ○ 3 Getting kinda toasty
- ○ 4 Pretty baked
- ○ 5 Life is beautiful
- ○ 6 Mmmmm, munchies
- ○ 7 Whoa! High as a kite
- ○ 8 Totally stoned
- ○ 9 What was I doing again?
- ○ 10 Have you ever really looked at your hand?

DATE	TIME	LOCATION

High notes (METHOD / STRAIN / CHARACTERISTICS):

_____

_____

_____

What am I feeling?

_____

_____

_____

What am I doing? / What am I eating?

_____

_____

_____

_____

What can I absolutely not forget, no matter what?

_____

_____

_____

Genius idea:

_____

_____

_____

Big question:

_____

_____

_____

Doodle

THC is the primary mind-altering chemical in marijuana and is most concentrated in the buds of the female cannabis plant.

How High Am I?

- ○ 1 Not at all
- ○ 2 Feeling a buzz
- ○ 3 Getting kinda toasty
- ○ 4 Pretty baked
- ○ 5 Life is beautiful
- ○ 6 Mmmmm, munchies
- ○ 7 Whoa! High as a kite
- ○ 8 Totally stoned
- ○ 9 What was I doing again?
- ○ 10 Have you ever really looked at your hand?

DATE	TIME	LOCATION

High notes (METHOD / STRAIN / CHARACTERISTICS):

_____

_____

_____

What am I feeling?

_____

_____

_____

What am I doing? / What am I eating?

_____

_____

_____

What can I absolutely not forget, no matter what?

_____

_____

_____

Genius idea:

_____

_____

_____

Big question:

_____

_____

_____

Doodle

The average life of a taste bud cell is ten days, so next time you get the munchies, pay attention to the details: the different tastes, smells, and textures of what you're eating.

How High Am I?

- ○ 1 Not at all
- ○ 2 Feeling a buzz
- ○ 3 Getting kinda toasty
- ○ 4 Pretty baked
- ○ 5 Life is beautiful
- ○ 6 Mmmmm, munchies
- ○ 7 Whoa! High as a kite
- ○ 8 Totally stoned
- ○ 9 What was I doing again?
- ○ 10 Have you ever really looked at your hand?

DATE	TIME	LOCATION

High notes (METHOD / STRAIN / CHARACTERISTICS):

_____

_____

_____

What am I feeling?

_____

_____

_____

What am I doing? / What am I eating?

_____

_____

_____

_____

What can I absolutely not forget, no matter what?

_____

_____

_____

Genius idea:

_____

_____

_____

Big question:

_____

_____

_____

Doodle

Store your weed in an airtight jar in a cool dark place to prevent your buds from drying out.

How High Am I?

○ 1 Not at all
○ 2 Feeling a buzz
○ 3 Getting kinda toasty
○ 4 Pretty baked
○ 5 Life is beautiful

○ 6 Mmmmm, munchies
○ 7 Whoa! High as a kite
○ 8 Totally stoned
○ 9 What was I doing again?
○ 10 Have you ever really looked at your hand?

DATE	TIME	LOCATION

High notes (METHOD / STRAIN / CHARACTERISTICS):

_____
_____
_____

What am I feeling?

_____
_____
_____

What am I doing? / What am I eating?

_____
_____
_____

What can I absolutely not forget, no matter what?

_____

_____

_____

Genius idea:

_____

_____

_____

Big question:

_____

_____

_____

Doodle

Hashish is a product of marijuana and is made by collecting and compressing the THC-rich resin from the buds of the female cannabis plant.

How High Am I?

- ○ 1 Not at all
- ○ 2 Feeling a buzz
- ○ 3 Getting kinda toasty
- ○ 4 Pretty baked
- ○ 5 Life is beautiful
- ○ 6 Mmmmm, munchies
- ○ 7 Whoa! High as a kite
- ○ 8 Totally stoned
- ○ 9 What was I doing again?
- ○ 10 Have you ever really looked at your hand?

DATE	TIME	LOCATION

High notes (METHOD / STRAIN / CHARACTERISTICS):

_____

_____

_____

What am I feeling?

_____

_____

_____

What am I doing? / What am I eating?

_____

_____

_____

What can I absolutely not forget, no matter what?

_____

_____

_____

Genius idea:

_____

_____

_____

Big question:

_____

_____

_____

Doodle

The first record of marijuana's medicinal properties dates as far back as 28 B.C. in an ancient Chinese pharmacopeia. Marijuana is still used today to alleviate pain, stimulate appetite, and treat a wide variety of ailments.

How High Am I?

- ○ 1 Not at all
- ○ 2 Feeling a buzz
- ○ 3 Getting kinda toasty
- ○ 4 Pretty baked
- ○ 5 Life is beautiful
- ○ 6 Mmmmm, munchies
- ○ 7 Whoa! High as a kite
- ○ 8 Totally stoned
- ○ 9 What was I doing again?
- ○ 10 Have you ever really looked at your hand?

DATE	TIME	LOCATION

High notes (METHOD / STRAIN / CHARACTERISTICS):

_____
_____
_____

What am I feeling?

_____
_____
_____

What am I doing? / What am I eating?

_____
_____
_____
_____

What can I absolutely not forget, no matter what?

_____
_____
_____

Genius idea:

_____
_____
_____

Big question:

_____
_____
_____

Doodle

It's high time to laugh every day. Studies show that it's good for you. Laughing relieves tension and stress, increases blood flow, boosts the immune system, and triggers the release of endorphins.

How High Am I?

- ○ 1 Not at all
- ○ 2 Feeling a buzz
- ○ 3 Getting kinda toasty
- ○ 4 Pretty baked
- ○ 5 Life is beautiful
- ○ 6 Mmmmm, munchies
- ○ 7 Whoa! High as a kite
- ○ 8 Totally stoned
- ○ 9 What was I doing again?
- ○ 10 Have you ever really looked at your hand?

DATE	TIME	LOCATION

High notes (METHOD / STRAIN / CHARACTERISTICS):

_____

_____

_____

What am I feeling?

_____

_____

_____

What am I doing? / What am I eating?

_____

_____

_____

What can I absolutely not forget, no matter what?

_____
_____
_____

Genius idea:

_____
_____
_____

Big question:

_____
_____
_____

Doodle

Marijuana has been used in religious and spiritual practices throughout history and is said to enhance communication with the spirit world.

How High Am I?

○ 1 Not at all
○ 2 Feeling a buzz
○ 3 Getting kinda toasty
○ 4 Pretty baked
○ 5 Life is beautiful

○ 6 Mmmmm, munchies
○ 7 Whoa! High as a kite
○ 8 Totally stoned
○ 9 What was I doing again?
○ 10 Have you ever really looked at your hand?

DATE	TIME	LOCATION

High notes (METHOD / STRAIN / CHARACTERISTICS):

_____
_____
_____

What am I feeling?

_____
_____
_____

What am I doing? / What am I eating?

_____
_____
_____

What can I absolutely not forget, no matter what?

_____

_____

_____

Genius idea:

_____

_____

_____

Big question:

_____

_____

_____

Doodle

It's high time to break your routine. Try something different and unusual. Do something that takes you out of your comfort zone. Challenge yourself. Learn something new.

How High Am I?

○ 1 Not at all
○ 2 Feeling a buzz
○ 3 Getting kinda toasty
○ 4 Pretty baked
○ 5 Life is beautiful

○ 6 Mmmmm, munchies
○ 7 Whoa! High as a kite
○ 8 Totally stoned
○ 9 What was I doing again?
○ 10 Have you ever really looked at your hand?

DATE	TIME	LOCATION

High notes (METHOD / STRAIN / CHARACTERISTICS):

_____
_____
_____

What am I feeling?

_____
_____
_____

What am I doing? / What am I eating?

_____
_____
_____
_____

What can I absolutely not forget, no matter what?

_____

_____

_____

Genius idea:

_____

_____

_____

Big question:

_____

_____

_____

Doodle

THC is the primary mind-altering chemical in marijuana and is most concentrated in the buds of the female cannabis plant.

How High Am I?

- ○ 1 Not at all
- ○ 2 Feeling a buzz
- ○ 3 Getting kinda toasty
- ○ 4 Pretty baked
- ○ 5 Life is beautiful
- ○ 6 Mmmmm, munchies
- ○ 7 Whoa! High as a kite
- ○ 8 Totally stoned
- ○ 9 What was I doing again?
- ○ 10 Have you ever really looked at your hand?

DATE	TIME	LOCATION

High notes (METHOD / STRAIN / CHARACTERISTICS):

_____

_____

_____

What am I feeling?

_____

_____

_____

What am I doing? / What am I eating?

_____

_____

_____

What can I absolutely not forget, no matter what?

_____

_____

_____

Genius idea:

_____

_____

_____

Big question:

_____

_____

_____

_____

Doodle

The average life of a taste bud cell is ten days, so next time you get the munchies, pay attention to the details: the different tastes, smells, and textures of what you're eating.

How High Am I?

- ○ 1 Not at all
- ○ 2 Feeling a buzz
- ○ 3 Getting kinda toasty
- ○ 4 Pretty baked
- ○ 5 Life is beautiful
- ○ 6 Mmmmm, munchies
- ○ 7 Whoa! High as a kite
- ○ 8 Totally stoned
- ○ 9 What was I doing again?
- ○ 10 Have you ever really looked at your hand?

DATE	TIME	LOCATION

High notes (METHOD / STRAIN / CHARACTERISTICS):

_____

_____

_____

What am I feeling?

_____

_____

_____

What am I doing? / What am I eating?

_____

_____

_____

What can I absolutely not forget, no matter what?

_____

_____

_____

Genius idea:

_____

_____

_____

Big question:

_____

_____

_____

Doodle

Store your weed in an airtight jar in a cool dark place to prevent your buds from drying out.

How High Am I?

- ○ 1 Not at all
- ○ 2 Feeling a buzz
- ○ 3 Getting kinda toasty
- ○ 4 Pretty baked
- ○ 5 Life is beautiful
- ○ 6 Mmmmm, munchies
- ○ 7 Whoa! High as a kite
- ○ 8 Totally stoned
- ○ 9 What was I doing again?
- ○ 10 Have you ever really looked at your hand?

DATE	TIME	LOCATION

High notes (METHOD / STRAIN / CHARACTERISTICS):

_____
_____
_____

What am I feeling?

_____
_____
_____

What am I doing? / What am I eating?

_____
_____
_____

What can I absolutely not forget, no matter what?

_____

_____

_____

Genius idea:

_____

_____

_____

Big question:

_____

_____

_____

Doodle

Hashish is a product of marijuana and is made by collecting and compressing the THC-rich resin from the buds of the female cannabis plant.

How High Am I?

- ○ 1 Not at all
- ○ 2 Feeling a buzz
- ○ 3 Getting kinda toasty
- ○ 4 Pretty baked
- ○ 5 Life is beautiful
- ○ 6 Mmmmm, munchies
- ○ 7 Whoa! High as a kite
- ○ 8 Totally stoned
- ○ 9 What was I doing again?
- ○ 10 Have you ever really looked at your hand?

DATE	TIME	LOCATION

High notes (METHOD / STRAIN / CHARACTERISTICS):

_____

_____

_____

What am I feeling?

_____

_____

_____

What am I doing? / What am I eating?

_____

_____

_____

What can I absolutely not forget, no matter what?

_____

_____

_____

Genius idea:

_____

_____

_____

Big question:

_____

_____

_____

Doodle

The first record of marijuana's medicinal properties dates as far back as 28 B.C. in an ancient Chinese pharmacopeia. Marijuana is still used today to alleviate pain, stimulate appetite, and treat a wide variety of ailments.

How High Am I?

- ◯ 1 Not at all
- ◯ 2 Feeling a buzz
- ◯ 3 Getting kinda toasty
- ◯ 4 Pretty baked
- ◯ 5 Life is beautiful
- ◯ 6 Mmmmm, munchies
- ◯ 7 Whoa! High as a kite
- ◯ 8 Totally stoned
- ◯ 9 What was I doing again?
- ◯ 10 Have you ever really looked at your hand?

DATE	TIME	LOCATION

High notes (METHOD / STRAIN / CHARACTERISTICS):

_____

_____

_____

What am I feeling?

_____

_____

_____

What am I doing? / What am I eating?

_____

_____

_____

What can I absolutely not forget, no matter what?

_____
_____
_____

Genius idea:

_____
_____
_____

Big question:

_____
_____
_____

Doodle

It's high time to laugh every day. Studies show that it's good for you. Laughing relieves tension and stress, increases blood flow, boosts the immune system, and triggers the release of endorphins.

How High Am I?

- ○ 1 Not at all
- ○ 2 Feeling a buzz
- ○ 3 Getting kinda toasty
- ○ 4 Pretty baked
- ○ 5 Life is beautiful
- ○ 6 Mmmmm, munchies
- ○ 7 Whoa! High as a kite
- ○ 8 Totally stoned
- ○ 9 What was I doing again?
- ○ 10 Have you ever really looked at your hand?

DATE	TIME	LOCATION

High notes (METHOD / STRAIN / CHARACTERISTICS):

_____

_____

_____

What am I feeling?

_____

_____

_____

What am I doing? / What am I eating?

_____

_____

_____

What can I absolutely not forget, no matter what?

_____

_____

_____

Genius idea:

_____

_____

_____

Big question:

_____

_____

_____

Doodle

Marijuana has been used in religious and spiritual practices throughout history and is said to enhance communication with the spirit world.

How High Am I?

- ◯ 1 Not at all
- ◯ 2 Feeling a buzz
- ◯ 3 Getting kinda toasty
- ◯ 4 Pretty baked
- ◯ 5 Life is beautiful
- ◯ 6 Mmmmm, munchies
- ◯ 7 Whoa! High as a kite
- ◯ 8 Totally stoned
- ◯ 9 What was I doing again?
- ◯ 10 Have you ever really looked at your hand?

DATE	TIME	LOCATION

High notes (METHOD / STRAIN / CHARACTERISTICS):

_____

_____

_____

What am I feeling?

_____

_____

_____

What am I doing? / What am I eating?

_____

_____

_____

What can I absolutely not forget, no matter what?

_____
_____
_____

Genius idea:

_____
_____
_____

Big question:

_____
_____
_____

Doodle

It's high time to break your routine. Try something different and unusual. Do something that takes you out of your comfort zone. Challenge yourself. Learn something new.

How High Am I?

- ○ 1 Not at all
- ○ 2 Feeling a buzz
- ○ 3 Getting kinda toasty
- ○ 4 Pretty baked
- ○ 5 Life is beautiful
- ○ 6 Mmmmm, munchies
- ○ 7 Whoa! High as a kite
- ○ 8 Totally stoned
- ○ 9 What was I doing again?
- ○ 10 Have you ever really looked at your hand?

DATE	TIME	LOCATION

High notes (METHOD / STRAIN / CHARACTERISTICS):

_____

_____

_____

What am I feeling?

_____

_____

_____

What am I doing? / What am I eating?

_____

_____

_____

What can I absolutely not forget, no matter what?

_____

_____

_____

Genius idea:

_____

_____

_____

Big question:

_____

_____

_____

Doodle

THC is the primary mind-altering chemical in marijuana and is most concentrated in the buds of the female cannabis plant.

How High Am I?

○ 1 Not at all
○ 2 Feeling a buzz
○ 3 Getting kinda toasty
○ 4 Pretty baked
○ 5 Life is beautiful
○ 6 Mmmmm, munchies
○ 7 Whoa! High as a kite
○ 8 Totally stoned
○ 9 What was I doing again?
○10 Have you ever really looked at your hand?

DATE	TIME	LOCATION

High notes (METHOD / STRAIN / CHARACTERISTICS):

_____
_____
_____

What am I feeling?

_____
_____
_____

What am I doing? / What am I eating?

_____
_____
_____
_____

What can I absolutely not forget, no matter what?

_____

_____

_____

Genius idea:

_____

_____

_____

Big question:

_____

_____

_____

Doodle

The average life of a taste bud cell is ten days, so next time you get the munchies, pay attention to the details: the different tastes, smells, and textures of what you're eating.

How High Am I?

- ○ 1 Not at all
- ○ 2 Feeling a buzz
- ○ 3 Getting kinda toasty
- ○ 4 Pretty baked
- ○ 5 Life is beautiful
- ○ 6 Mmmmm, munchies
- ○ 7 Whoa! High as a kite
- ○ 8 Totally stoned
- ○ 9 What was I doing again?
- ○ 10 Have you ever really looked at your hand?

DATE	TIME	LOCATION

High notes (METHOD / STRAIN / CHARACTERISTICS):

_____

_____

_____

What am I feeling?

_____

_____

_____

What am I doing? / What am I eating?

_____

_____

_____

What can I absolutely not forget, no matter what?

_____

_____

_____

Genius idea:

_____

_____

_____

Big question:

_____

_____

_____

Doodle

Store your weed in an airtight jar in a cool dark place to prevent your buds from drying out.

How High Am I?

- ○ 1 Not at all
- ○ 2 Feeling a buzz
- ○ 3 Getting kinda toasty
- ○ 4 Pretty baked
- ○ 5 Life is beautiful
- ○ 6 Mmmmm, munchies
- ○ 7 Whoa! High as a kite
- ○ 8 Totally stoned
- ○ 9 What was I doing again?
- ○ 10 Have you ever really looked at your hand?

DATE	TIME	LOCATION

High notes (METHOD / STRAIN / CHARACTERISTICS):

_____

_____

_____

What am I feeling?

_____

_____

_____

What am I doing? / What am I eating?

_____

_____

_____

What can I absolutely not forget, no matter what?

_____

_____

_____

Genius idea:

_____

_____

_____

Big question:

_____

_____

_____

_____

Doodle

Hashish is a product of marijuana and is made by collecting and compressing the THC-rich resin from the buds of the female cannabis plant.

How High Am I?

- ○ 1 Not at all
- ○ 2 Feeling a buzz
- ○ 3 Getting kinda toasty
- ○ 4 Pretty baked
- ○ 5 Life is beautiful
- ○ 6 Mmmmm, munchies
- ○ 7 Whoa! High as a kite
- ○ 8 Totally stoned
- ○ 9 What was I doing again?
- ○ 10 Have you ever really looked at your hand?

| DATE | TIME | LOCATION |

High notes (METHOD / STRAIN / CHARACTERISTICS):

_____

_____

_____

What am I feeling?

_____

_____

_____

What am I doing? / What am I eating?

_____

_____

_____

What can I absolutely not forget, no matter what?

_____

_____

_____

Genius idea:

_____

_____

_____

Big question:

_____

_____

_____

Doodle

The first record of marijuana's medicinal properties dates as far back as 28 B.C. in an ancient Chinese pharmacopeia. Marijuana is still used today to alleviate pain, stimulate appetite, and treat a wide variety of ailments.

How High Am I?

- ○ 1 Not at all
- ○ 2 Feeling a buzz
- ○ 3 Getting kinda toasty
- ○ 4 Pretty baked
- ○ 5 Life is beautiful
- ○ 6 Mmmmm, munchies
- ○ 7 Whoa! High as a kite
- ○ 8 Totally stoned
- ○ 9 What was I doing again?
- ○10 Have you ever really looked at your hand?

DATE	TIME	LOCATION

High notes (METHOD / STRAIN / CHARACTERISTICS):

_____

_____

_____

What am I feeling?

_____

_____

_____

What am I doing? / What am I eating?

_____

_____

_____

What can I absolutely not forget, no matter what?

_____

_____

_____

Genius idea:

_____

_____

_____

Big question:

_____

_____

_____

Doodle

It's high time to laugh every day. Studies show that it's good for you. Laughing relieves tension and stress, increases blood flow, boosts the immune system, and triggers the release of endorphins.

How High Am I?

- ○ 1 Not at all
- ○ 2 Feeling a buzz
- ○ 3 Getting kinda toasty
- ○ 4 Pretty baked
- ○ 5 Life is beautiful
- ○ 6 Mmmmm, munchies
- ○ 7 Whoa! High as a kite
- ○ 8 Totally stoned
- ○ 9 What was I doing again?
- ○ 10 Have you ever really looked at your hand?

DATE	TIME	LOCATION

High notes (METHOD / STRAIN / CHARACTERISTICS):

_____

_____

_____

What am I feeling?

_____

_____

_____

What am I doing? / What am I eating?

_____

_____

_____

_____

What can I absolutely not forget, no matter what?

_____

_____

_____

Genius idea:

_____

_____

_____

Big question:

_____

_____

_____

Doodle

Marijuana has been used in religious and spiritual practices throughout history and is said to enhance communication with the spirit world.

How High Am I?

○ 1 Not at all
○ 2 Feeling a buzz
○ 3 Getting kinda toasty
○ 4 Pretty baked
○ 5 Life is beautiful

○ 6 Mmmmm, munchies
○ 7 Whoa! High as a kite
○ 8 Totally stoned
○ 9 What was I doing again?
○ 10 Have you ever really looked at your hand?

DATE	TIME	LOCATION

High notes (METHOD / STRAIN / CHARACTERISTICS):

_____
_____
_____

What am I feeling?

_____
_____
_____

What am I doing? / What am I eating?

_____
_____
_____

What can I absolutely not forget, no matter what?

_____

_____

_____

Genius idea:

_____

_____

_____

Big question:

_____

_____

_____

Doodle

It's high time to break your routine. Try something different and unusual. Do something that takes you out of your comfort zone. Challenge yourself. Learn something new.

How High Am I?

- ○ 1 Not at all
- ○ 2 Feeling a buzz
- ○ 3 Getting kinda toasty
- ○ 4 Pretty baked
- ○ 5 Life is beautiful
- ○ 6 Mmmmm, munchies
- ○ 7 Whoa! High as a kite
- ○ 8 Totally stoned
- ○ 9 What was I doing again?
- ○ 10 Have you ever really looked at your hand?

DATE	TIME	LOCATION

High notes (METHOD / STRAIN / CHARACTERISTICS):

_____

_____

_____

What am I feeling?

_____

_____

_____

What am I doing? / What am I eating?

_____

_____

_____

_____

What can I absolutely not forget, no matter what?

_____
_____
_____

Genius idea:

_____
_____
_____

Big question:

_____
_____
_____

Doodle

THC is the primary mind-altering chemical in marijuana and is most concentrated in the buds of the female cannabis plant.

How High Am I?

- ○ 1 Not at all
- ○ 2 Feeling a buzz
- ○ 3 Getting kinda toasty
- ○ 4 Pretty baked
- ○ 5 Life is beautiful
- ○ 6 Mmmmm, munchies
- ○ 7 Whoa! High as a kite
- ○ 8 Totally stoned
- ○ 9 What was I doing again?
- ○ 10 Have you ever really looked at your hand?

DATE	TIME	LOCATION

High notes (METHOD / STRAIN / CHARACTERISTICS):

_____

_____

_____

What am I feeling?

_____

_____

_____

What am I doing? / What am I eating?

_____

_____

_____

What can I absolutely not forget, no matter what?

_____

_____

_____

Genius idea:

_____

_____

_____

Big question:

_____

_____

_____

Doodle

The average life of a taste bud cell is ten days, so next time you get the munchies, pay attention to the details: the different tastes, smells, and textures of what you're eating.

How High Am I?

- ○ 1 Not at all
- ○ 2 Feeling a buzz
- ○ 3 Getting kinda toasty
- ○ 4 Pretty baked
- ○ 5 Life is beautiful
- ○ 6 Mmmmm, munchies
- ○ 7 Whoa! High as a kite
- ○ 8 Totally stoned
- ○ 9 What was I doing again?
- ○ 10 Have you ever really looked at your hand?

DATE	TIME	LOCATION

High notes (METHOD / STRAIN / CHARACTERISTICS):

_____

_____

_____

What am I feeling?

_____

_____

_____

What am I doing? / What am I eating?

_____

_____

_____

What can I absolutely not forget, no matter what?

_____

_____

_____

Genius idea:

_____

_____

_____

Big question:

_____

_____

_____

Doodle

Store your weed in an airtight jar in a cool dark place to prevent your buds from drying out.

How High Am I?

- ○ 1 Not at all
- ○ 2 Feeling a buzz
- ○ 3 Getting kinda toasty
- ○ 4 Pretty baked
- ○ 5 Life is beautiful
- ○ 6 Mmmmm, munchies
- ○ 7 Whoa! High as a kite
- ○ 8 Totally stoned
- ○ 9 What was I doing again?
- ○ 10 Have you ever really looked at your hand?

DATE	TIME	LOCATION

High notes (METHOD / STRAIN / CHARACTERISTICS):

_____

_____

_____

What am I feeling?

_____

_____

_____

What am I doing? / What am I eating?

_____

_____

_____

What can I absolutely not forget, no matter what?

_____

_____

_____

Genius idea:

_____

_____

_____

Big question:

_____

_____

_____

Doodle

Hashish is a product of marijuana and is made by collecting and compressing the THC-rich resin from the buds of the female cannabis plant.

How High Am I?

- ○ 1 Not at all
- ○ 2 Feeling a buzz
- ○ 3 Getting kinda toasty
- ○ 4 Pretty baked
- ○ 5 Life is beautiful
- ○ 6 Mmmmm, munchies
- ○ 7 Whoa! High as a kite
- ○ 8 Totally stoned
- ○ 9 What was I doing again?
- ○ 10 Have you ever really looked at your hand?

DATE	TIME	LOCATION

High notes (METHOD / STRAIN / CHARACTERISTICS):

_____

_____

_____

What am I feeling?

_____

_____

_____

What am I doing? / What am I eating?

_____

_____

_____

What can I absolutely not forget, no matter what?

_____

_____

_____

Genius idea:

_____

_____

_____

Big question:

_____

_____

_____

Doodle

The first record of marijuana's medicinal properties dates as far back as 28 B.C. in an ancient Chinese pharmacopeia. Marijuana is still used today to alleviate pain, stimulate appetite, and treat a wide variety of ailments.

How High Am I?

- ○ 1 Not at all
- ○ 2 Feeling a buzz
- ○ 3 Getting kinda toasty
- ○ 4 Pretty baked
- ○ 5 Life is beautiful
- ○ 6 Mmmmm, munchies
- ○ 7 Whoa! High as a kite
- ○ 8 Totally stoned
- ○ 9 What was I doing again?
- ○ 10 Have you ever really looked at your hand?

DATE	TIME	LOCATION

High notes (METHOD / STRAIN / CHARACTERISTICS):

_____

_____

_____

What am I feeling?

_____

_____

_____

What am I doing? / What am I eating?

_____

_____

_____

_____

What can I absolutely not forget, no matter what?

_____

_____

_____

Genius idea:

_____

_____

_____

Big question:

_____

_____

_____

Doodle

It's high time to laugh every day. Studies show that it's good for you.
Laughing relieves tension and stress, increases blood flow, boosts the
immune system, and triggers the release of endorphins.

How High Am I?

- ○ 1 Not at all
- ○ 2 Feeling a buzz
- ○ 3 Getting kinda toasty
- ○ 4 Pretty baked
- ○ 5 Life is beautiful

- ○ 6 Mmmmm, munchies
- ○ 7 Whoa! High as a kite
- ○ 8 Totally stoned
- ○ 9 What was I doing again?
- ○ 10 Have you ever really looked at your hand?

DATE	TIME	LOCATION

High notes (METHOD / STRAIN / CHARACTERISTICS):

_____

_____

_____

What am I feeling?

_____

_____

_____

What am I doing? / What am I eating?

_____

_____

_____

What can I absolutely not forget, no matter what?

_____

_____

_____

Genius idea:

_____

_____

_____

Big question:

_____

_____

_____

Doodle

Marijuana has been used in religious and spiritual practices throughout history and is said to enhance communication with the spirit world.

How High Am I?

- ○ 1 Not at all
- ○ 2 Feeling a buzz
- ○ 3 Getting kinda toasty
- ○ 4 Pretty baked
- ○ 5 Life is beautiful
- ○ 6 Mmmmm, munchies
- ○ 7 Whoa! High as a kite
- ○ 8 Totally stoned
- ○ 9 What was I doing again?
- ○ 10 Have you ever really looked at your hand?

DATE	TIME	LOCATION

High notes (METHOD / STRAIN / CHARACTERISTICS):

_____

_____

_____

What am I feeling?

_____

_____

_____

What am I doing? / What am I eating?

_____

_____

_____

What can I absolutely not forget, no matter what?

_____

_____

_____

Genius idea:

_____

_____

_____

Big question:

_____

_____

_____

Doodle

It's high time to break your routine. Try something different and unusual. Do something that takes you out of your comfort zone. Challenge yourself. Learn something new.

How High Am I?

- ○ 1 Not at all
- ○ 2 Feeling a buzz
- ○ 3 Getting kinda toasty
- ○ 4 Pretty baked
- ○ 5 Life is beautiful
- ○ 6 Mmmmm, munchies
- ○ 7 Whoa! High as a kite
- ○ 8 Totally stoned
- ○ 9 What was I doing again?
- ○ 10 Have you ever really looked at your hand?

DATE	TIME	LOCATION

High notes (METHOD / STRAIN / CHARACTERISTICS):

_____

_____

_____

What am I feeling?

_____

_____

_____

What am I doing? / What am I eating?

_____

_____

_____

What can I absolutely not forget, no matter what?

_____
_____
_____

Genius idea:

_____
_____
_____

Big question:

_____
_____
_____

Doodle

THC is the primary mind-altering chemical in marijuana and is most concentrated in the buds of the female cannabis plant.

How High Am I?

- ○ 1 Not at all
- ○ 2 Feeling a buzz
- ○ 3 Getting kinda toasty
- ○ 4 Pretty baked
- ○ 5 Life is beautiful
- ○ 6 Mmmmm, munchies
- ○ 7 Whoa! High as a kite
- ○ 8 Totally stoned
- ○ 9 What was I doing again?
- ○ 10 Have you ever really looked at your hand?

DATE	TIME	LOCATION

High notes (METHOD / STRAIN / CHARACTERISTICS):

_____

_____

_____

What am I feeling?

_____

_____

_____

What am I doing? / What am I eating?

_____

_____

_____

What can I absolutely not forget, no matter what?

_____

_____

_____

Genius idea:

_____

_____

_____

Big question:

_____

_____

_____

Doodle

The average life of a taste bud cell is ten days, so next time you get the munchies, pay attention to the details: the different tastes, smells, and textures of what you're eating.

How High Am I?

○ 1 Not at all
○ 2 Feeling a buzz
○ 3 Getting kinda toasty
○ 4 Pretty baked
○ 5 Life is beautiful

○ 6 Mmmmm, munchies
○ 7 Whoa! High as a kite
○ 8 Totally stoned
○ 9 What was I doing again?
○ 10 Have you ever really looked at your hand?

DATE	TIME	LOCATION

High notes (METHOD / STRAIN / CHARACTERISTICS):

_____

_____

_____

What am I feeling?

_____

_____

_____

What am I doing? / What am I eating?

_____

_____

_____

What can I absolutely not forget, no matter what?

_____

_____

_____

Genius idea:

_____

_____

_____

Big question:

_____

_____

_____

Doodle

Store your weed in an airtight jar in a cool dark place to prevent your buds from drying out.

How High Am I?

- ○ 1 Not at all
- ○ 2 Feeling a buzz
- ○ 3 Getting kinda toasty
- ○ 4 Pretty baked
- ○ 5 Life is beautiful
- ○ 6 Mmmmm, munchies
- ○ 7 Whoa! High as a kite
- ○ 8 Totally stoned
- ○ 9 What was I doing again?
- ○ 10 Have you ever really looked at your hand?

DATE	TIME	LOCATION

High notes (METHOD / STRAIN / CHARACTERISTICS):

_____
_____
_____

What am I feeling?

_____
_____
_____

What am I doing? / What am I eating?

_____
_____
_____
_____

What can I absolutely not forget, no matter what?

_____
_____
_____

Genius idea:

_____
_____
_____

Big question:

_____
_____
_____

Doodle

Hashish is a product of marijuana and is made by collecting and compressing the THC-rich resin from the buds of the female cannabis plant.

How High Am I?

○ 1 Not at all
○ 2 Feeling a buzz
○ 3 Getting kinda toasty
○ 4 Pretty baked
○ 5 Life is beautiful
○ 6 Mmmmm, munchies
○ 7 Whoa! High as a kite
○ 8 Totally stoned
○ 9 What was I doing again?
○ 10 Have you ever really looked at your hand?

DATE	TIME	LOCATION

High notes (METHOD / STRAIN / CHARACTERISTICS):

_____
_____
_____

What am I feeling?

_____
_____
_____

What am I doing? / What am I eating?

_____
_____
_____
_____

What can I absolutely not forget, no matter what?

_____

_____

_____

Genius idea:

_____

_____

_____

Big question:

_____

_____

_____

Doodle

The first record of marijuana's medicinal properties dates as far back as 28 B.C. in an ancient Chinese pharmacopeia. Marijuana is still used today to alleviate pain, stimulate appetite, and treat a wide variety of ailments.